MARGATE'S SEASID

Published by English Heritage, Kemble Drive, Swindon SN2 2GZ
www.english-heritage.org.uk
English Heritage is the Government's statutory adviser on all aspects of the historic environment.

© English Heritage 2007

Printing 10 9 8 7 6 5 4 3 2 1

Images (except as otherwise shown) © English Heritage, © English Heritage. NMR or © Crown
copyright. NMR.

First published 2007

ISBN 978 1 905624 66 9
Product code 51335

British Library Cataloguing in Publication Data
A CIP catalogue record for this book is available from the British Library.

Application for the reproduction of images should be made to the National Monuments Record. Every
effort has been made to trace the copyright holders and we apologise in advance for any unintentional
omissions, which we would be pleased to correct in any subsequent edition of this book.

The National Monuments Record is the public archive of English Heritage. For more information,
contact NMR Enquiry and Research Services, National Monuments Record Centre, Kemble Drive,
Swindon SN2 2GZ; telephone (01793) 414600.

Brought to publication by Rachel Howard, Publishing, English Heritage.
Page layout by Swales & Willis Ltd, Exeter.
Printed in the UK by Cambridge Printing.

Front cover
*The first of Margate's outdoor tidal
pools, the bathing pool at Cliftonville,
opened in 1927. It became known as
Margate Lido during the 1930s and
continued to provide an important
bathing facility until it closed in 1977
and was in-filled. [AA046231]*

Inside front cover
*Fronting the harbour, The Parade was
formerly Margate's premier location for
visitor amenities. It contained hotels,
shops, baths and a library, and was a
fashionable promenade. [OP00641]*

MARGATE'S SEASIDE HERITAGE

Nigel Barker, Allan Brodie, Nick Dermott, Lucy Jessop and Gary Winter

Cliftonville & Sands Margate. 3337. W. & Co. L.td

Contents

Frontispiece
The eastern expansion of Margate was so extensive that it became known as Margate New Town and later Cliftonville. As well as developing a social distinction, the high chalk cliffs provided a scenic contrast to the low-lying seafront around the harbour.
[OP00623]

Acknowledgements

The historical section of this book is based on fieldwork and research conducted by Nigel Barker, Allan Brodie, Dr Lucy Jessop and Gary Winter of English Heritage, and Nick Dermott of Thanet District Council. Dr Andy Brown, John Cattell, Colum Giles and Barry Jones kindly read the manuscript and offered useful comments. The contemporary photographs were taken by Peter Williams, and Mike Hesketh-Roberts undertook the onerous task of making the project team's photographs compatible with the National Monument Record's systems. The map on the inside back cover was prepared by Tony Berry. Other help, in various forms, was provided by Ursula Dugard-Craig, Cynthia Howell, Irene Peacock and the National Monuments Record darkroom staff. Adrian Pepin provided the 1927 panoramic view of Margate from his large collection of images of Thanet (http://wpd.co.uk). While every effort has been made to trace copyright holders of some images, we apologise to any whom we have not been able to contact.

During our numerous visits we have been consistently and enthusiastically welcomed and helped by many people who work and live in Margate. In particular we would like to express our grateful thanks to Jane De Bliek at Paigle Properties Ltd, David Hannaford formerly at Margate Library, Terry Meech at Margate Museum, Colin Norwood at Arlington House, Adrian Pepin at Media House, Sarah Vickery at the Shell Grotto, Michael Wheatley-Ward formerly at the Theatre Royal and Julie Wickendon at Drapers Homes.

Foreword

Margate is one of England's first seaside resorts. Since the early 18th century, people have been visiting the town to bathe in the sea, first for health reasons, but in more recent years for pleasure and a change of scenery. The presence of visitors transformed this once small working coastal town into a playground for some of the wealthiest members of London society. However, as it was located along the Thames from the capital, Margate has always attracted a wide range of visitors and was selected as the site of the world's first sea-bathing hospital.

Although the seaside retains the affection of most people, it is no longer the primary destination for holidaymakers. Competition from European destinations has had a particularly strong impact on Margate where, in the late 20th century, many of the attractions and major hotels closed and much of its historic old town has been neglected. However, new policies supported by public and private investment indicate that the signs of this decline have been recognised and are being reversed.

At the heart of revitalising any seaside resort should be an appreciation of the historic character of the place. Three centuries of holidays have left behind a rich tapestry of buildings and this legacy has been little understood and often undervalued. Well-maintained historic buildings can contribute to making a town a pleasant place to live, work and visit. This book describes the colourful history of the seaside holiday at Margate and the buildings that survive to tell this story. It also demonstrates that these valuable parts of our past can once again play a part in the town's future.

Dr Simon Thurley, Chief Executive of English Heritage
Councillor Sandy Ezekiel, Leader of Thanet District Council

Sea Front Margate. 3331. W & Co. Ld.

CHAPTER 1

Introduction

The seaside holiday and the seaside resort are two of England's greatest exports to the world. Since the early 18th century, when some of the wealthiest people first sought improved health by bathing in saltwater, the lure of the sea has been a fundamental part of the British way of life, and millions of people still head to the coast each year.

Margate has an important place in the story of seaside holidays. It vies with Scarborough, Whitby and Brighton for the title of England's first seaside resort, and it was the first to offer sea-water baths to visitors. Margate can also claim other firsts, including the first Georgian square built at a seaside resort (Cecil Square), the first substantial seaside development outside the footprint of an historic coastal town, the site of the world's first sea-bathing hospital, and, as a result of its location along the Thames from London, the first popular resort frequented by middle- and lower-middle-class holidaymakers.

Until the mid-19th century Margate was at the forefront of the discovery of the seaside, but with the arrival of railways, visitors who had been restricted to travelling along the Thames could now explore stretches of coast further afield. However, by the eve of the First World War, Margate was as busy as any resort, with the exception of perhaps Brighton and Blackpool. The small-scale, intimate facilities provided for hundreds of Georgian visitors were replaced by large hotels and new forms of entertainment for the hundreds of thousands of holidaymakers and trippers who arrived each year. The prosperity of the seaside continued until the 1960s, but with growing leisure time, increased disposable income and easy access to foreign holidays, all seaside resorts have suffered decline, though none has probably suffered as much as Margate.

Margate's character, fashioned by changing seaside vogues, reflects the story of the English taste for health and recreation by the sea. The old town is at the heart of the settlement, adjacent to the harbour, the focus of the town's prosperity before the arrival of the holidaymakers: the streets are narrow; the blocks of development small in area; there is none of the regularity of later centuries. In the last quarter of the 18th century, development, driven by the tastes and expectations of well-to-do visitors, took place inland around Margate's two Georgian squares. Fashionable

Margate Seafront, c1890–1910. Observed from Marine Gardens, sea bathing from bathing machines at high tide makes for popular viewing by visitors along Marine Terrace and Marine Drive. [OP00632]

new homes modelled on London examples were used to house growing numbers of visitors in the heart of the expanding resort. In the early 19th century new development began to spread along the coast, creating the dense urban fabric of Westbrook and Cliftonville. With tall sea-facing terraces along the coast and smaller terraces leading inland, Cliftonville became the favoured domain for prosperous middle-class visitors. In the 20th century, the outward expansion of Margate continued through the creation of large areas of suburbia with a range of bungalows and more substantial houses, leading to its physical, and administrative, merger with neighbouring settlements along the coast.

Margate's expansion was rapid in the 18th and early 19th centuries and has left behind concrete remains. The same can be said of its recent decline. The town was the setting for Pawel Pawlikowski's stark but romantic film *Last Resort* (2000), and has become a by-word in the media for rundown seaside resorts. Critical commentators can find obvious signs of decay, but they often overlook the town's rich heritage and the great potential that it offers for the future.

Margate has experienced a vicious circle, with decreasing visitor numbers leading to reduced investment and consequently poorer facilities that again attract fewer holidaymakers. To break this cycle requires knowledge, money, courage and faith, qualities that are now beginning to emerge. A re-evaluation of Margate's history and heritage will be a key factor in its future. Celebrating the past can help to shape the future. Through understanding the historic environment of Margate and its contribution to a sense of place, it is possible to stimulate people to value and care for it; a significant stimulus for social and economic renewal.

The late 20th century was a period of apparently constant gloom for Margate, yet the town and its extraordinarily welcoming people have a resilience that suggests the future will be brighter. The Royal Sea Bathing Hospital, which stood empty for a decade, became a prominent symbol of decay confronting visitors arriving by car, but it is now being converted into up-market apartments. The Turner Contemporary gallery on the seafront Rendezvous site beside the lifeboat station is envisaged as a flagship for the reinvention of the old town as an artistic quarter. Neglected sites – such as Dreamland, and the shopping centre and car park around Arlington House – offer huge potential for appropriate redevelopment, and decisions that are now being made will help to shape the future of the town.

It is unlikely that Margate will ever attract the vast numbers of visitors that flocked there in the 19th and early 20th centuries. However, with growing concerns about the environmental effects of air travel and a continuing awareness of the threat of excessive exposure to the sun, the English seaside holiday may enjoy some form of revival. If Margate finds ways to renew itself while retaining its historic identity, it may once again become a vibrant destination for holidays, as well as being an attractive place for people to live and work.

CHAPTER 2

'Merry Margate': its seaside story

Margate in 1736

1736 was the pivotal year in Margate's history. Reverend John Lewis published the second edition of his history of the Isle of Thanet, which included a plan/birds-eye view of the town (Fig 1), and a notice appeared in a Kent newspaper advertising Margate's first sea-water bath. These two events were unrelated – one summarised the past, the other hinted at the future – but what they reveal is that Margate was beginning the transition from a small working town into a fashionable seaside resort.

In 1586 William Camden had described the people of Thanet as: 'excessively industrious, getting their living like amphibious animals both by sea and land'. Depending on the time of year, 'they make nets, catch codd, herrings and mackerel, &c. make trading voyages, manure their land, plough, sow, harrow, reap, and store their corn, expert in both professions'.[1] However, by the early 18th century parts of the town's fishing industry had gone into decline. In the first edition of Lewis's book, published in 1723, he described a struggling fishing industry, but by 1736 the situation had worsened; some people involved with the North-Sea fishery, having met with little success in preceding years, had given up fishing.

Margate's prosperity had depended on its harbour, as the base for a fishing fleet and as an outlet for agricultural produce from the Isle of Thanet. At the time of John Leland's visit in the 1530s the pier was in 'great disrepair' and in 1662 'this Pier and Harbour was much ruinated and decayed'.[2] On Lewis's map it was depicted as a long, timber structure with a reversed-L plan, with a lamp and crane at the seaward end and a warehouse at the landward end.

In 1565 Margate had been a small town with only 108 houses, and Reverend Lewis's view 150 years later suggests that the town had grown little. It was still huddled around the edge of the sea, with houses ranged along the coast from the base of the pier to where Marine Drive was later created. Houses had also been built along three main streets running inland: King Street, Market Street and the High Street. Although Lewis's view may be naïve in its perspective, it appears to be a generally accurate and vivid depiction of the town.

Cliftonville Sands, c1890–1910. In contrast to Margate Sands, the beaches at Cliftonville sit at the foot of dramatic chalk cliffs. Accessed via natural fissures in the cliff, the beaches were popular for bathing, taking the air and promenading. [OP00640]

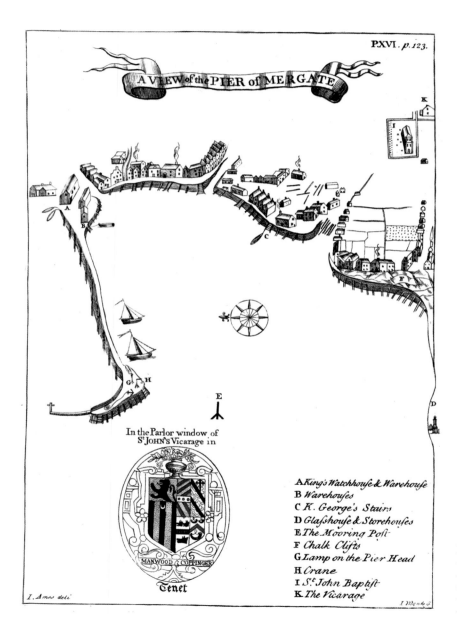

Figure 1 *This view from Lewis's book reveals how in c1736 Margate was clustered around the pier, its major source of wealth. There is no hint of the fledgling resort activities that would alter the town over the ensuing 250 years. [DP017639 Society of Antiquaries of London]*

John Macky described Margate in the early 18th century as 'a poor pitiful Place' and Lewis described it as 'irregularly built, and the Houses generally old and low'.[3] A handful of buildings survive to provide a glimpse of Margate before its transformation into a resort. The Tudor House in King Street is a 16th-century, timber-framed house, its elaborate form and framing indicating that it was the home of a wealthy citizen (Fig 2). A number of other early timber-framed buildings in King Street appear to have been re-fronted in the 18th century. Other readily

Figure 2 *King Street, once a main road to Broadstairs, contains some of the town's oldest surviving dwellings, including Tudor House, a close-studded, continuous jettied, timber-framed house. [AA046458]*

available building materials were also used. In King Street there is a two-storied house dating from the 1680s faced in knapped flint with brick dressings (Fig 3), and in Lombard Street a late 17th-century brick building is decorated with small brick arches and pilasters (Fig 4). The earliest buildings in Margate survive in the streets around the Market Place, the heart of the historic town. In keeping with the antiquity of its origins, this part of Margate has relatively narrow streets and the blocks are small in area.

The first visitors arrive 1730–1769

Reverend Lewis's book provides a vivid picture of Margate's past, but it contains no hint of the momentous changes that were beginning to take place. In 1736 an advertisement for a sea-water bath appeared in a local newspaper:

> Whereas Bathing in Sea-Water has for several Years, and by great numbers of People, been found to be of great Service in many Chronical Cases, but for want of a convenient and private Bathing Place, many of

Figure 3 (above, left) *29–31 King Street show something of the vernacular style of houses prior to the external influences that transformed Margate into a seaside health and leisure resort. Particularly picturesque are the shaped end gables of these houses that were built in the late 17th and early 18th centuries. [AA050591]*

Figure 4 (above, right) *8–9 Lombard Street, a prestigious house when it was built in the late 17th century, contrasts sharply with the towering form of the neighbouring houses constructed a century later. [AA050156]*

both Sexes have not cared to expose themselves to the open Air; This is to inform all Persons, that Thomas Barber, Carpenter, at Margate in the Isle of Thanett, hath lately made a very convenient Bath, into which the Sea Water runs through a Canal about 15 Foot long. You descend into the Bath from a private Room adjoining to it.[4]

The opening words claim that sea bathing had been practised 'for several Years' and by 'great numbers of People'. This might explain why in 1730 Margate had been able to attract a theatre company from Canterbury during the summer. Visitors were being drawn to Margate by the prospect of improving their health, and elsewhere there is evidence of a growing interest in sea water as a health treatment. By the 1730s sea bathing was being practised at Liverpool, Whitby, Scarborough and Brighton, and on the Lincolnshire coast, but Margate was the first coastal town known to have provided a substantial, purpose-built sea-water bath. Scarborough, the site of a spa since 1626, already had significant facilities that could be used by bathers, and other spas such as Epsom, Tunbridge Wells and Bath also seem to have served as a model for the way that new seaside resorts developed.

Margate also has a special place in the history of another key feature of the seaside: the bathing machine. This mobile changing room was used to take people out into the sea, and once suitably immersed the bathers would 'enjoy' a dip, sometimes with a guide to help them. The first reference to a primitive version of these contraptions dates from the 1720s and an engraving of Scarborough of 1735 provides the earliest depiction of one. At Margate Zechariah Brazier was said to have been the first guide to have taken a bather into the sea in a 'simple machine, a cart'.[5] However, the key event occurred in 1753, when Benjamin Beale invented the modesty hood. This canvas canopy could be lowered and raised by the driver of the machine, allowing bathers a modicum of privacy as well as some protection from wind and waves (Fig 5).

The popularity of sea bathing in the 18th century meant that there were too few bathing machines to cater for all bathers at any time. Therefore a number of bathing rooms were created on the High Street where prospective bathers could drink sea water, read newspapers, enjoy

Figure 5 *The antiquarian Joseph Ames inserted this drawing into a copy of Reverend Lewis's book, which he deposited in the Society of Antiquaries in the 1750s. It is the earliest depiction of a bathing machine with modesty hood and the first description of how 'bathing waggons' operated. [DP017642 Society of Antiquaries of London]*

conversation and even play the piano while they waited for a bathing machine. The first two bathing rooms seem to have been established in the 1750s; by 1763 there were three, served by eleven bathing machines and by 1797 seven were recorded. Some of these waiting rooms were developed into bath-houses during the late 18th century, with Hughes' Bathing Room in 1797 providing heated, sea-water baths. A major storm in 1808 destroyed these facilities, but their utility and popularity were demonstrated by the fact that new ones were built in their place (Fig 6). Although these buildings have now disappeared, they have left their imprint on the west side of the lower end of the High Street where a series of single-storied shops echo the form of the small bathing rooms that existed there 200 years ago (Figs 7 and 8).

Other developments in the third quarter of the 18th century demonstrate how Margate was being transformed into a resort. To cater for visitors, claimed a guidebook, 'Some good Houses have been built within a few years, and others are building: The old ones daily receive all the improvements they are capable of.'[6] This was a response to the

Figure 6 *The rebuilt High Street bathing rooms, with their perilous stairs down to the sea, are clearly shown in this engraving of 1812. The return elevation of Philpot's establishment advertises 'warm salt water baths and machines for bathing'. [DP022308]*

Figures 7 and 8 These images of the High Street reveal the evolution of the area before and after the erection of buildings on Marine Drive. The low-level form of the bathing rooms can still be seen in their later replacements. However, the tall buildings constructed on Marine Drive block the views that were previously enjoyed from the balconied houses on the east side of the High Street. [BB67/08933; AA046470]

growing number of wealthy visitors who were seeking more comfortable and more fashionable lodgings. By 1770 a later edition of the same guidebook could claim that 'There are several good Lodging-houses, and their Rooms, though frequently small, are neat. They may be said to be commodious too, if it is considered that many are now applied to a Use for which they were not originally intended. However, many have been built of late Years, expressly with an Intention of their being hired for Lodgings'.[7]

New development was concentrated within the footprint of the original town, along the early streets and around the Market Place. In King Street a number of early timber-framed houses were raised, rendered and under-built to create passable imitations of stylish Georgian townhouses. As well as buildings that were being updated, a few new ones were erected. On the south side of the market there is a three-storied, single-bay-wide building, with a shop on the ground floor. It stands out from nearby buildings because, although Georgian in form,

11

its façade is finished with knapped flint, a reflection of earlier, vernacular traditions (Fig 9).

One new building of the 1760s stands out in Margate, and would have been exceptional in any contemporary seaside resort. Captain John Gould, a wealthy tea-planter from India, returned to England in 1766 and settled in Margate, where he built India House in Hawley Street. Reputed to be a copy of the house he occupied in Calcutta, it is double-piled: a single-storied front pile with two stories in the block behind (Fig 10). Captain Gould is perhaps the earliest recorded example of someone retiring to the seaside, and during the 19th and 20th centuries retirement to the sea, in England and abroad, became a dream for many people.

As well as bathing facilities and houses, new residents and visitors required entertainment. However, concern about the longevity of the popularity of the seaside holiday meant that people were not prepared to invest significant sums of money in new purpose-built facilities. In

Figure 9 (below, left) *The Olde Cabin Antiques, 15 Market Place. Situated between two brick houses, this property combines contemporary forms with vernacular materials. [AA050541]*

Figure 10 (below, right) *India House, 12 Hawley Street. One of Margate's more remarkable houses, India House contrasts sharply with the form and style of dwellings constructed in nearby Cecil Square and Hawley Square, suggesting it was intended as a family home rather than a house that could be let as lodgings for visitors. [AA050169]*

1763 the principal venue – the New Inn, run by Mr Mitchener – included a large room that was used for assemblies. Theatrical entertainment had been available, at least sporadically, since 1730, and by the 1750s theatre companies, or troupes of comedians, were returning annually. By 1761 they were able to use a permanent theatre, a converted barn in the Dane. In 1771 a new theatre was created in a stable at the rear of the Fountain Inn and this remained the sole playhouse for more than a decade.

One feature that seems to date from this period is the Shell Grotto, though whether it was originally open to the public is unknown. This mysterious structure was 'discovered' in 1835 and has been attributed to the Phoenicians and Romans. However, it seems to resemble an underground excavation, possibly created for extracting flint. Shell grottos enjoyed a particular vogue in the mid-18th century and many of the arrangements of shells seem to echo 18th-century architectural forms, such as fielded panelling, enlarged keystones, and gothic and ogee arches (Fig 11). A 1760 song may contain an oblique reference to this grotto:

> For views, lo, the Pier, and for walks the Parade;
> For coolness the Beach, and the Rope Walk for shade:
> Nor can Tunbridge, so fam'd for its rockwork and ware,
> With our cliffs, and our grottos, and shell-work compare.[8]

This probably refers to shell-work decoration on souvenirs, but the association of grottos and shell-work in the same line of a poem does seem to be a conscious reference to important features of the early resort.

By the end of the 1760s, Margate, like the other early resorts, was welcoming growing numbers of visitors, who were being crammed into some new houses, though normally they were accommodated in existing, but refurbished, homes within the area of the original town. Entertainment facilities were similarly rudimentary, even primitive, but it is clear that a lively social scene was beginning to exert its influence on the town and its facilities.

1769–1800 – a change of pace

The construction of Cecil Square ushered in a new phase in the story
of the seaside. It was the first case of landowners and businessmen
collaborating to develop a large scheme, the first new square to be built
at a seaside resort, and the earliest example of a significant development
outside the area of the historic town. Visitors were now arriving at
Margate in sufficient numbers, and perhaps more importantly returning
year after year, to make such a large investment worthwhile.

Cecil Square, originally known as the New Square, was laid out in
1769 by 'Mr Cecil', Sir John Shaw, Sir Edward Hales and several other
gentlemen. This date is recorded in several early guidebooks and on
a datestone at the north-east corner of the square (Fig 12), though a

Figure 11 *Comprising 2,000 square feet (186m^2)of
shell-covered walls, the Shell Grotto has intrigued
visitors to Margate for around 170 years. The
continuing debates surrounding the Grotto's origins
have ensured that its mysterious allure persists.
[AL0022/035/03/OP]*

Figure 12 *A plaque attached to Stockwell House at the north-east corner of Cecil Square celebrates the date of this important seaside development.* [AA049251]

guidebook of 1770 noted that building work was still in progress. The new square contained large houses built for fashionable families, a row of shops, and the purpose-built Assembly Rooms and circulating library that had been erected beside Fox's Tavern (Figs 13, 14 and 15). Hawley Square was created by Sir Henry Hawley soon after Cecil Square (Fig 16). Building work may have begun in the 1770s, but the library in the north-west corner and the theatre in the north-east corner were built in 1786 and 1787 respectively, suggesting that most building work on the square dated from the 1780s (Fig 17).

These new squares were in marked contrast to the High Street, which was described in 1793 as 'a long dirty lane, consisting chiefly of malthouses, herring hangs and poor little cottages of fishermen', though some new houses were improving it.[9] Most houses being erected around

Figure 13 (above) *Cecil Square was a residential, commercial and entertainment centre for the wealthy visitors of a new seaside resort. The square has always been a busy traffic hub, but it is now entirely occupied by a car park and the main road.* [AA049298]

ROYAL HOTEL & ASSEMBLY ROOMS.

Figure 14 (left) *Royal Hotel and Assembly Rooms in c1827. From the early development of Cecil Square until the demolition of The Hippodrome, the south-eastern corner of the square was the site of leisure and entertainment facilities in Margate. The Assembly Room on the first floor is demarcated by the double-height Venetian windows.* [Courtesy of Margate Library Local History Collection, Kent Libraries and Archives]

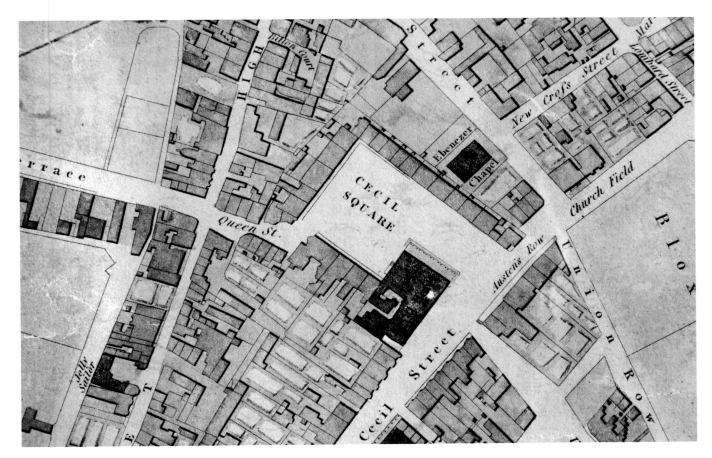

Figure 15 *Edmunds' Plan shows that Cecil Square had been completed by 1821. Far from being a secluded residential development, Cecil Square was also a transport hub connecting the old town with new developments on the coast. [DP032186 Courtesy of Margate Museum]*

Figure 16 (above) *Unlike Cecil Square, Hawley Square was built around an enclosed 'pleasure ground' garden. In 1800 the square comprised 'an entire range of genteel houses from one end of it to the other, most of which command a fine and extensive prospect over the sea'.* [DP032187 Courtesy of Margate Museum, from Edmunds' Plan]

Figure 17 (left) *The library in Hawley Square was built for Joseph Hall by Mr Crofts. It was described in an early guidebook as exceeding its main rival in 'size and magnificence'. The exterior elevations were surrounded by a colonnade that echoed the north elevation of the nearby Assembly Rooms.* [Courtesy of Margate Library Local History Collection, Kent Libraries and Archives]

1800 were in a standard Georgian form, sometimes with balconies opening from their first-floor rooms (Fig 18). Early guidebooks suggest that the new houses resembled contemporary buildings in parts of London and Westminster, but it might be more accurate to describe them as similar to homes in London's rapidly growing suburbs. For a town of Margate's size and distance from the capital, the number of large, four-storied houses is impressive. This is partly a mark of the status of its residents and visitors, but it is also a reflection of an economic fact of life. Tall buildings provided more rooms to rent out as lodgings and therefore more income for the owners. This type of income was not a major factor in towns that did not have to cater for large numbers of visitors, but it did have a marked impact on the size of houses in seaside towns.

The growing number of visitors also required new entertainment facilities. As well as the bathing rooms, they expected to find versions of the types of entertainment that could be enjoyed in London and Bath. The new Assembly Room was the centre of the social scene and there were also circulating libraries at the foot of the High Street, on the east side of Cecil Square and on Hawley Square. The Hawley Square library was the grandest built in Margate and arguably one of the finest ever built at a seaside resort (Fig 19). The other major Georgian entertainment facility was the Theatre Royal in Hawley Square. It was originally a simple brick building, its current appearance dating from a major reconstruction in 1874 (Fig 20). As well as entertainment in the town, visitors could travel out to nearby gardens, farms and small country houses. Dandelion, the site of a former manor house, was probably the most famous of these. It was attracting visitors in 1760, and an 1802 guidebook described how people enjoyed public breakfasts there twice a week, played bowls, danced to music provided by a band and played on a swing. As well as frequenting formal institutions for entertaining visitors, many people happily spent hours enjoying the beach, going on boat trips or riding donkeys. Many of the essentials of the modern seaside holiday were already in place by 1800 and even war with nearby France does not seem to have interrupted the social life of the rapidly growing resort.

Figure 18 *Houses on the south side of Hawley Square. Despite the general uniformity of many of the houses built here, the piecemeal development can be clearly discerned by the differing storey levels and phase joints between houses. [AA050144]*

Figure 19 *The Hawley Square library comprised a shop selling goods and a library, separated by a row of six Corinthian columns. In 1820 the library was 'generally filled with personages of rank and fashion' and was also a venue for card games and music recitals. [Courtesy of Margate Library Local History Collection, Kent Libraries and Archives]*

BETTISON'S LIBRARY, MARGATE.

THE THEATRE.

Figure 20 *The Theatre Royal, on the corner of Addington Street and Hawley Square, opened in 1787 and cost £4,000 to build. It is shown here in its early incarnation, before the theatre was revamped in the 1870s. [DP017645 Society of Antiquaries of London, from Kidd 1831,67]*

In the late 18th century Margate was popular with large numbers of affluent visitors, but it was also chosen as the location for a sea-bathing hospital to treat poor people suffering from scrofula (tuberculosis of the glands, joints and bones), the first hospital of its kind in the world. Dr John Coakley Lettsom, a successful and philanthropic doctor practising in London, was the driving force behind its creation and by May 1796 the building was ready to receive its first 30 patients. Reverend John Pridden designed the building with open loggias beside nine- and six-bedded wards on either side of a two-storied staff and administration block (Fig 21).

Although fresh air and sun were used as treatments, sea bathing was the main means of curing patients. Dr John Anderson, a physician at the hospital, published *A Practical Essay on the Good and Bad Effects of Sea-Water and Sea-Bathing* in 1795. Like other 18th-century writers, he claimed that a huge range of conditions could be treated by sea-water

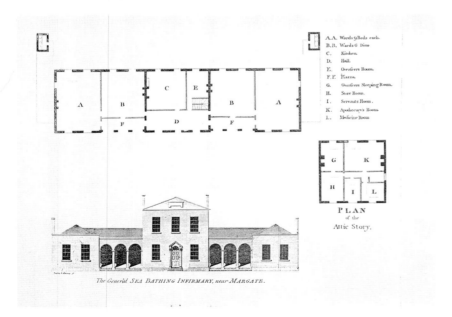

A.A. Wards 9 Beds each.
B.B. Wards 6 Ditto
C.   Kitchen.
D.   Hall.
E.   Overseers Room.
F.F. Piazza.
G.   Overseers Sleeping Room.
H.   Store Room.
I.   Servants Room.
K.   Apothecary's Room.
L.   Medicine Room

PLAN
of the
Attic Story.

The General SEA BATHING INFIRMARY, near MARGATE.

Figure 21 *The plans and elevation of the original Royal Sea Bathing Hospital show how Lettsom's and Pridden's concept for the treatment of scrofula was translated into a purpose-built hospital design. The ground-floor rooms interconnect and all four wards are well lit, heated and have access to the piazzas, the loggias in front of the building. [BB94/19942]*

bathing, including rheumatism, scurvy, leprosy, rickets and various common infections. Patients were taken to the sea and fully immersed using the hospital's bathing machine, though this treatment was unsuitable for most of the year.

The hospital grew rapidly during the 19th century, so that at the 1841 census it was treating 214 patients (Fig 22). Indoor baths containing salt-water were established in 1858, replacing sea bathing and allowing year-round treatment. In 1910 the swimming bath was converted into a ward, marking the end of bathing in water as a means to cure patients. The hospital became part of the National Health Service on 4 July 1948, and continued in use until its closure in July 1996 (Fig 23). The buildings are being converted into luxury apartments (*see* Fig 68).

THE

ROYAL SEA BATHING INFIRMARY

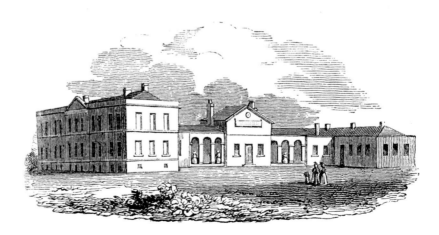

Figure 22 *This view of the Royal Sea Bathing Hospital in 1831 shows the early 19th-century additions to the north and south, which enabled it to accommodate over 200 patients. [DP017648 Society of Antiquaries of London, from Kidd 1831]*

Figure 23 *Taken from the top of the former nurses'
home, this view gives an impression of the extensive
development of the Royal Sea Bathing Hospital site
immediately before it closed in July 1996.
[BB91/21379]*

Why Margate – location, location, location?

Margate's early origin as a resort, its popularity for 200 years and the character of its visitors were all heavily dependent on its location. It was favoured by early health-seeking tourists because of its good transport links with London, and as transport improved, and became cheaper, the numbers of visitors grew and their character changed.

Stagecoaches were the principal way of reaching seaside resorts in the 18th century. In 1771, visitors from London had to take a coach to Canterbury where they changed on to services to Margate, a journey time of around thirteen to fourteen hours, but by 1815 direct services from London had been established.

What made Margate unusual among the earliest resorts was that a substantial proportion, perhaps the majority, of its visitors arrived by sea. An 1810 guidebook noted that Margate was 'conveniently stationed in respect to the metropolis for conveyance by water or land', and Margate's location influenced the founders of the Royal Sea Bathing Hospital.[10] Hoys, single-masted ships weighing between 60 and 100 tons, sailed between London and Margate, transporting grain from the Isle of Thanet to London, and returning with goods such as coal and timber. Gradually passengers and their luggage displaced the cargo, and dedicated sailing packets developed. Hoys were cheaper than travelling by coach and on a good day they made the journey in a shorter time. In the 1790s a single coach trip to Margate cost between 21s and 26s, while the cheapest hoy fare was only 5s, allowing a lower class of visitor to travel to Margate.

This extension of the holiday habit accelerated with the introduction of a regular steamer service in 1815 (Fig 24). This initially reduced the journey time to a guaranteed eight hours, and by 1840 it had been further shortened to six and a half hours. Steamers were faster, larger and cheaper, leading to decreased fares and greater numbers of passengers, so that between 1815 and 1835 the number of people arriving each year by sea rose from 22,000 to 109,000. As the speed of steamers increased during the mid-19th century, men were able to remain in London during the week and join their families at weekends on the so-called 'husbands' boats'.

Figure 24 *The Steam Yacht 'The Thames' began a regular service between London and Margate in 1815. [Courtesy of Margate Library Local History Collection, Kent Libraries and Archives]*

Margate's pier was essential to the town's success. The Improvement Act of 1787 contained a provision for rebuilding the pier in stone, though a guidebook in 1809 still referred to it as being wooden, as if the early structure had just been clad in stone. The 1808 storm caused severe damage and it was rebuilt between 1810 and 1815, though large numbers of people still arrived by sea during this hiatus. The pier is approximately 900ft long (274m) and is roughly half-octagonal in plan (Figs 25 and 26). Initially this renewed structure still had to deal with passengers and cargo, but in 1824 Jarvis' Jetty, a 1,186ft-long (356m) wooden structure was added to the east of the pier, its length allowing passengers to land irrespective of the state of the tide. At Margate new 'piers' added in the 19th century bore the name 'jetty' to avoid confusion with the harbour's stone pier.

Margate's ease of access from London helped to shape the type of visitors it attracted. Like Brighton, it was frequented by dukes and duchesses, and lords and ladies, but not in the same numbers. Instead guidebooks, songs and poems refer, not always flatteringly, to the range

Figure 25 *Edmunds' 1821 plan shows the recently rebuilt harbour pier. The outer edge of the pier was raised to form a fashionable promenade above the harbourside where ships were landing passengers and cargo.* [DP032184 Courtesy of Margate Museum]

Figure 26 *The harbour pier is approximately 900ft long, 60ft wide and 26ft high (274m long, 18m wide, 8m high) and is built of roughly dressed stone. Margate's pier was essential to its development as a seaside resort and though it is now used by fewer boats, it still remains a significant presence on the seafront.* [DP032181]

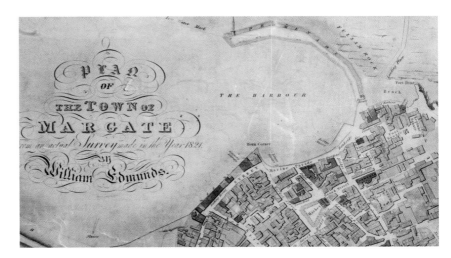

of Margate's visitors. This became more obvious after steamers were introduced, but there was evidence of Margate's social diversity as early as the mid-18th century. George Keate, describing Margate in the early 1760s wrote that:

> The decent tradesman slips from town for his half crown, and strolls up and down the Parade as much at ease as he treads his own shop. – His wife, who perhaps never eloped so far from the metropolis before, stares with wonder at the many new objects which surround her . . . The farmer's rosy-cheeked daughter crosses the island on her pillion, impatient to peep at the London females . . . . The Londoner views with a disdainful surprise, the awkward straw hat, and exposed ruddy countenance of the rustic nymph; who in turn scrutinizes the inexplicable coiffure of her criticiser, unable to conceive what can have befallen the features of a face of which the nose is the only visible sign.[11]

Margate might have been acquiring buildings worthy of comparison with some of the better buildings being built in London, but the varying standard of people occupying these houses in the summer, classified by the first guidebooks as 'High and Low, Rich and Poor, Sick and Sound', gave Margate its distinctive character in the Georgian period.[12]

1800–1846 – development along the coast

Margate's population rose by 65 per cent between 1801 and 1821, from 4,766 to 7,843. In the same period England's population increased by 35 per cent and Kent's by 37 per cent. Although Margate was relatively small in 1801, its rate of growth was still impressive. In 1800, development was concentrated near the heart of the original town, but by the early 19th century a fundamental shift in this pattern was taking place. Edmunds' map of 1821 demonstrates that new developments were being erected on previously undeveloped land along the coast on either side of the historic town. Buenos Ayres, a terrace of 13 houses, was begun in 1803 to the west of the town (Figs 27 and 28). 'The New Road', now

Figure 27 *Edmunds' 1821 plan reveals that, despite having been started in 1803, Buenos Ayres had not been completed nearly twenty years later, with space for another two houses still remaining. [DP032183 Courtesy of Margate Museum]*

Figure 28 *Buenos Ayres was the earliest major terraced house development laid out between the Royal Sea Bathing Hospital and the town. The original Georgian fenestration has been replaced by canted bay windows that rise through two, three or four storeys. [AA049285]*

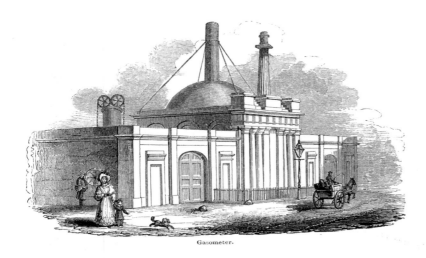

Gasometer.

Figure 29 *The neoclassical style gasworks in King Street was built in 1824 to provide the gas for Margate's street lighting. [DP017644 Society of Antiquaries of London, from Kidd 1831]*

Marine Terrace, was built in 1809 to link Cecil Square to Buenos Ayres, and the first houses were established at its east end, beside the old town. By 1821 the first buildings in Cliftonville had also been erected to the east of the Fort.

To cater for the rapidly growing population, many new facilities were required. The Improvement Act of 1787 included provisions for the paving, lighting and general improvement of the town, and it created a body of Commissioners who were responsible for improving the town and running many of its new services. In 1821 they built the town hall, including a prison, and gas lighting was introduced in 1824. The gas was contained in a gasometer within the gasworks in King Street described as a 'neat and elegant building in the Dane, built after a Grecian mode'.[13] It was a symbol of a town embracing modern developments and therefore featured in an 1831 guidebook as a building of interest (Fig 29). To improve the water supply, public water pumps were erected in 1826. A good, clean water supply and modern facilities were essential if visitors were to be attracted to resorts.

By the time the railway arrived at Margate, the small, struggling, working town of a century earlier was growing into a mature, popular seaside resort, favoured particularly by middle-class and lower-middle-class visitors from London. In most resorts, the arrival of the railway ushered in a period of rapid expansion, but the creation of the network throughout southern England actually led to a slight reverse in Margate's fortunes. The growing ease of railway travel encouraged the exploration of resorts further afield and cancelled out the advantages that Margate had enjoyed because of its location on the Thames. However, by the end of the 19th century, Margate would again be growing as rapidly as most resorts around the coast.

Margate's terraced houses

The builders of Margate's earliest planned developments were seeking to create houses that were suitable for visitors to use as lodgings. In appearance these new buildings were seeking to emulate the latest London fashions.

Figure 30 (right) *Doric doorcase, Cecil Square. Similar examples can be found throughout London, including in Queen Anne's Gate (1770–71) and Colebrooke Row (1771–72). [DP039323]*

Figure 31 (far right) *Rusticated doorcase, Union Crescent. This example reflects a simplified version of the elaborate vermiculated surrounds used in Bedford Square, London (1776–86). [DP026088]*

Cecil Square's plain Georgian houses (1769), with well-proportioned Doric doorcases, echo houses in areas of the capital that developed between 1750 and 1775, such as Westminster or Islington (Fig 30). The use of stock brick in Hawley Square (1770s–1780s) makes the similarities to London more explicit, and the rusticated, stuccoed door-surrounds of Union Crescent (1799) mimic those of Bedford Square in Bloomsbury (1776–86) (Fig 31). Margate's new domestic buildings originally employed strict Georgian forms, though their exteriors were usually softened during the 19th century by the addition of balconies and bay windows (Fig 32).

Margate's principal architectural allegiance was to London's suburbs, but occasionally other influences can be detected. The stuccoed bows and Ionic orders of Fort Lodge (1825–30) recall contemporary developments in Brighton, especially Brunswick Square (1820s) (Fig 33). Fort Paragon

Figure 32 *The double-pile, four-storied houses of Union Crescent are typically Georgian in form: each house is three bays wide, with sash windows diminishing in height storey by storey. They remained popular high-class residences into the mid-19th century. [DP026090]*

Figure 33 (opposite) *Temeraire Court, 33–36 Fort Crescent, was originally built as part of a terrace of Regency houses, bringing an unexpected taste of Brighton to Margate. [DP039329]*

(1830), with canopied balconies, is a later adaptation of the basic London design blended with touches of the elegant terraces of Brighton or Cheltenham (Fig 34).

The second half of the 19th century saw Margate grow in two main directions: westward into Westbrook and eastward into Cliftonville. To the west, Royal Crescent (1850s) brought a new standard of development to the town, with its fashionable curved plan and Italianate window forms; its best façade faces the sea and is embellished with Composite pilasters and ironwork balconies (Fig 35).

Figure 34 *The former glories of Fort Paragon, now mostly stuccoed and clad with utilitarian ironwork balconies, can still be seen in the two houses at the south end of the terrace. These retain the original form of the delicate canopy and supports, as well as some exposed brickwork. [DP039328]*

Figure 35 *The large houses of Royal Crescent still retain much of their elegant exposed brickwork with elaborate stucco detail. [DP023147]*

Cliftonville's first development on a grand scale was Ethelbert Crescent in the 1860s with the Cliftonville Hotel as its centrepiece (Fig 36). It continued the Italianate theme, but with the addition of alternating Ionic porches and bays on the ground floor supporting undulating iron balconies. Sea View Terrace in Westbrook (before 1874) is a simplified version, with three rather than four storeys, Doric porches, and a veranda running the length of the terrace (Fig 37).

Much of Cliftonville's development from the 1870s onwards was inland, streets being built southwards from the seafront towards the

Figure 36 (above) *Ethelbert Crescent and the now demolished Cliftonville Hotel were the new face of Margate in the 1860s, promoting the sophisticated Cliftonville area with its own beaches and promenades as a more sedate and classy alternative to boisterous central Margate. [DP023148]*

Figure 37 (left) *Sea View Terrace, Westbrook, shares many similar features with Ethelbert Crescent – including the form of the top storey and cornice above – suggesting that they could be by the same architect or builder. [DP032160]*

Figure 38 (opposite, top) *Dalby Square, west side. The name Dalby Terrace and the date 1870 can still be seen in the face of the parapet. It was named after the builder Thomas Dalby Reeve, who served as mayor of Margate 1873–75. [AA050184]*

Figure 39 (opposite, bottom) *Dalby Square, east side. This pleasing variation on the theme of full-height bays is uninterrupted by porches or balconies but unified by terracotta detailing and handsome dentilated cornices. [DP032178]*

expanding Northdown Road. Many of these terraces had multi-storey bay windows, often rising to the full height of each house. Two designs of this type can be seen in Dalby Square, where sea views were possible, if rather limited (Fig 38 and 39). Numbers 10–15 (1870) retain the bay, columnar porch, and veranda arrangement of the best sea-view terraces but the bays rise through three of the four storeys. Numbers 25–32 (before 1872) have full-height bays undulating along the terrace. This type of design proved so popular that it was reproduced and refined throughout the next decades.

'Merry Margate'

The railway age dawned in Margate with the opening of Margate Sands station in 1846, followed in 1863 by the nearby Margate West, the site of the present station. Travellers were deposited close to the beach and Marine Drive, to the west of the historic centre, shifting the development of accommodation and entertainment away from the old town. The recently constructed houses of Marine Terrace had become lodging houses by the 1850s. Westbrook, convenient for both stations, expanded quickly, and by the mid-1870s standard mid-Victorian terraces of homes and lodging houses had infilled the area between Buenos Ayres and the Royal Sea Bathing Hospital.

Simultaneously, development in Cliftonville, east of the old town, dramatically increased the accommodation for residents and visitors. The Cliftonville Hotel, Margate's first grand hotel, was constructed in an Italianate style in 1868 beside Dalby Square (Figs 40 and 41). Even the rebuilding of the White Hart in 1882 on the Parade could not challenge its position as Margate's best hotel. Further large hotels were built at the turn of the century, including the Endcliffe and the Cliftonville Hydro, but the last to be constructed, and the last still operating, is the Walpole Bay Hotel, erected in 1914 (Fig 42). Cliftonville offered a higher quality of holiday and living experience, as its hotels, bathing platforms and beaches under the cliffs were not readily accessible from the station for day trippers.

Figure 40 *The Cliftonville Hotel, built in 1868, was a luxurious addition to Margate's visitor accommodation. Its position in Ethelbert Crescent allowed views over the cliff-top gardens to Newgate Promenade and easy access to the sea. [BL22782]*

Figure 41 *The Palm Court at the Cliftonville Hotel provided an elegant setting for socialising and relaxing under a delicate ironwork roof. [BL22784]*

Figure 42 *The Walpole Bay Hotel (1914), with its balconies, veranda, and public rooms, continues to offer visitors gracious seaside relaxation in the otherwise vanished tradition of the grand Cliftonville hotels.* [DP039334]

Figure 43 *The construction of Marine Drive in 1878–80 completed the road along the seafront. The present buildings, many of which are now unoccupied, predominantly date from the late 19th and early 20th centuries. [DP032206]*

Substantial investment in Margate's infrastructure during the second half of the 19th century enabled the town to keep pace with growing visitor numbers. In 1857, the Margate Waterworks Company opened a pumping station in Tivoli, and the waterworks were consistently updated during the next 50 years. The sewage system was improved around 1890, an event featured in guidebooks to boost public confidence in the town's healthiness. The sea walls were also strengthened and Marine Drive was created in 1878–80, but this reclamation on the new seafront isolated the bathing rooms on the High Street from the sea (Fig 43). Around 1900, a tramway was built along the seafront and through the town centre, connecting Margate with Broadstairs, Ramsgate, Westgate and Birchington. However, the most prominent Victorian addition to the town was the building of the Jetty, an iron successor to Jarvis's wooden

jetty. It was designed by Eugenius Birch to handle the large number of people disembarking from large steamers. The first of Birch's many piers, it opened in 1855 and was the first built using the screw-pile construction method (Figs 44 and 45).

As well as the new pier, a number of new and exciting attractions were added to complement the assembly room, theatre and libraries that survived from the Georgian period. The Hall by the Sea, located on the seafront, was established by the self-proclaimed 'Lord' George Sanger, the circus and entertainment entrepreneur. He created a palace of dining and dancing with pleasure gardens, an 'abbey' and a menagerie. The Hall by the Sea was replaced in 1898 with a spectacular purpose-built ballroom designed by Richard Dalby-Reeve (Fig 46). In 1920 this site acquired the name Dreamland, by which it is still known. The Marine Palace was built on reclaimed land at the base of the Jetty. This large structure, designed by Alfred Bedbrough in 1876, provided two swimming baths and an aquarium, as well as attractive seafront spaces for dancing and concerts. The Assembly Rooms, destroyed by fire, was replaced in 1898 by the larger New Theatre (later called the Hippodrome), which provided competition for the renovated Theatre Royal.

Figure 44 (above, left) *Birch's Jetty of 1855 was an instantly popular feature of the Victorian resort, serving as a landing place and a favourite promenade for visitors. [BB88/04260]*

Figure 45 (above, right) *The hexagonal pier head, which was added to the Jetty, opened in 1877. A bandstand, pavilion with cupola, and several kiosks provided entertainment and refreshments for the many passengers and promenaders. [OP00650]*

Figure 46 *This photograph of the florid fin-de-siècle rebuilding of the Hall by the Sea was taken soon after it was renamed Dreamland in 1920. [BB84/00899]*

Visitors also flocked in increasing numbers to the beaches, promenades and gardens. Minstrel troupes, such as Uncle Bones', entertained visitors on the sands (Fig 47). By the end of the 1890s, there were bandstands at the Fort, on the Jetty, and in Dane Park. Cafés, restaurants, shops and hotels lined the seafront, and the High Street was teeming with trippers. A guidebook of 1899–1900 considered that 'If, sometimes, the fun is a little noisy, perhaps even a trifle vulgar, who, after all, is the worse for it?'[14] Margate had long been christened 'Merry' in the press, with a reputation for the vulgarity of its lower-class patrons, but as the guidebook rightly claimed: 'there are at least two Margates, and that the Cliftonville and New Town quarters have scarcely anything in common with the regions sacred to the tripper.'[15]

Figure 47 *Margate's sandy beach, easily accessible from the railway stations, was often packed with trippers. Here, men, women and children, sporting hats and bonnets, are entertained by a minstrel show.* [OP00621]

Expansion and optimism – Margate before the Second World War

Margate's growth continued during the first half of the 20th century, with its population rising from 26,734 in 1901 to 36,742 in 1939. Cliftonville grew eastwards to West Northdown, while Eastern Esplanade extended into Palm Bay Avenue to become home to some examples of domestic Modernism (Fig 48). To the west, Westbrook no longer appeared as an isolated settlement as it expanded westwards towards the neighbouring resort of Westgate-on-Sea and southwards towards Garlinge. In 1935 Margate's boundaries were extended to include the resorts of Westgate-on-Sea and Birchington, almost doubling the area of the borough and increasing the population to around 41,000.

In the early 20th century Margate offered a range of modern facilities. The most successful entertainment building was arguably

Figure 48 *These two houses in Palm Bay Avenue are good examples of the types of modernist houses that were built on seafront roads in many resorts during the 1930s. [DP023149]*

PAVILION AND WINTER GARDENS, CLIFTONVILLE.

the Winter Gardens, a product of municipal foresight and confidence (Fig 49). Constructed in less than a year, it opened in August 1911 and provided the kind of year-round concert facilities that had not been available since the demise of the Assembly Rooms. Technological advances also played a role in changing the face of mass entertainment, particularly in the creation of cinemas and amusement-park rides. Margate can still boast two early, surviving cinemas: the Parade Cinema, opposite the pier, opened in 1911 and the former Cinema de Luxe was built at the top of the High Street in 1914–15 (Fig 50). At Dreamland the Scenic Railway (1919–20) now stands as a forlorn reminder of the many exciting rides that once existed (Figs 51 and 52). The present Dreamland Cinema of 1935, styled on Berlin's 1928 Titania Palast, could originally accommodate an audience of 2,200 (Fig 53). These very different remains all point to the original inter-war vibrancy of Margate and Dreamland.

Leisure activities focused on fresh air, swimming and sunbathing were particularly popular throughout Europe in the inter-war years, and Margate boasted an impressive array of facilities to cater for this.

Figure 49 (above, left) *The Winter Gardens was built by excavating into Fort Green. The complex was designed to host indoor and outdoor concerts, and was home to the resort's Municipal Orchestra. [PC07755]*

Figure 50 (above, right) *When it opened in June 1911, the Parade Cinema could accommodate 600 cinemagoers in its single-level hall. It became a bingo hall in the 1960s, and was later converted into a snooker club. [AA050229]*

Figure 51 (opposite) *Taken in April 1951, this aerial photograph shows the Dreamland site and the wealth of rides and stalls that existed after the Second World War. [RAF/58/619/5052 English Heritage (NMR) RAF Photography]*

The Marine Terrace Bathing Pavilion and the Cliftonville Bathing Pool (later known as Margate Lido) opened in 1926 and 1927 respectively (Fig 54). More basic tidal pools were added to the seaward side of the Marine Terrace Bathing Pavilion, and at Walpole Bay, both opening on 18 June 1937. There was also a smaller tidal bathing pool off Marine Drive, directly opposite the site of the former High Street Bathing Rooms. With some irony, the inspiration for much of the modern outdoor health culture came from Germany, the same nation that brought this era to an abrupt end.

While Dreamland was the largest alteration to the west of the old town, slum clearance for the Fort Road Improvement Scheme was the major change for the eastern part of the old town. This area was the

Figure 52 (opposite, top) *Viewed from Arlington House, the Scenic Railway and other surviving Dreamland structures now appear rather forsaken within a sea of concrete. [DP032138]*

Figure 53 (opposite, bottom) *The last of Julian Leathart and WF Granger's cinema designs, the new Dreamland cinema was built to entice visitors to the amusement park behind. The slim fin tower, which echoed recent Berlin cinema designs, was also adopted by cinemas in the Odeon chain. [CC47/00761]*

Figure 54 (above) *The inter-war modernisation of the Clifton Baths site included the construction of an open-air, tidal swimming pool that later took up the fashionable 'Lido' epithet. Only three lidos remain open on the coast of England: at Penzance, Plymouth and Saltdean. [AA046227]*

location of modest, functional buildings supporting the port and fishing activities, interspersed with cheap cafés and souvenir shops for Victorian visitors arriving by steamer (Fig 55). By the 1930s these buildings were largely boarded up. Therefore, in 1934, in response to the national slum-clearance programme required by The Housing Act of 1930, Margate Borough Council proposed the clearance of the narrow streets and derelict properties on Fort Road. In their place a short section of dual carriageway was built, creating a significant physical and psychological barrier between the old town and the harbour (Figs 56 and 57).

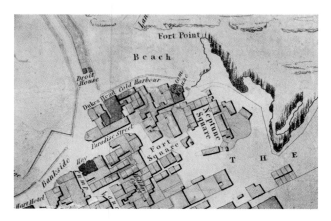

Figure 55 *Edmunds' Plan of 1821 shows the area that was cleared as part of the Fort Road Improvement Scheme. [DP032194 Courtesy of Margate Museum]*

Figures 56 and 57 *The 1927 and 2007 views reveal the extent of change over time. Not only have prominent landmarks been lost, the townscape has been altered, particularly as a result of the Fort Road Improvement Scheme on the left. [Courtesy of Adrian Pepin, Media House; DP023151]*

Storm and stagnation – the decline of the resort infrastructure

Margate's location made it vulnerable to attack in wartime. During the Second World War more than 2,700 bombs and shells hit the town, destroying 238 buildings and damaging nearly 9,000 others (Fig 58). Perhaps more significant was the damage caused by depopulation. With the threat of invasion, the town's population dropped to around 10,000. An article published in *The Times* on 31 August 1943 noted that: 'From being a bright and well-kept background to cheerful holidaymaking, Margate has become damaged and shabby . . .'.[16] Before the war there were 30 first-class hotels, 60 smaller hotels, 150 private hotels, 1,300 boarding houses, 1,500 apartment houses and 3,500 private dwellings that took in visitors. In August 1943 there were just two hotels and a handful of boarding houses.

Figure 58 *Built as the centrepiece to the Trinity Square residential development, Holy Trinity Church had a 57ft-high (17m-high) nave and a tower that rose to a height of 136ft (41m). This evocative image taken shortly after the air raid of 1 June 1943 shows the extent of the damage. [AA43/07427]*

In August 1944 visitor restrictions to the Isle of Thanet were lifted and the population rose to around 19,000. However, Margate never regained its reputation with the kind of clientele that had frequented the large Victorian and Edwardian hotels of Cliftonville. Despite the purchase of six hotels by Butlins from 1955, which were collectively marketed as The Cliftonville Hotels, none survive. Three of the last of the Butlins hotels were combined to form the Grand Hotel, but retirement flats have now been built on this site.

The storm surge of 31 January–1 February 1953 is considered the worst peacetime disaster ever suffered in Britain, and it caused severe damage to Margate's resort infrastructure. The Westbrook Pavilion, Marine Terrace Bathing Pavilion, the Lido and the Jetty were damaged, and the bathing pavilions and cafés situated in the bays of Cliftonville were completely destroyed. A second catastrophic storm in 1978 marked the final demise of the Jetty, as well as other piers on the east coast of England.

The immediate post-war period was dominated by loss and decline, but the most prominent and controversial addition to the town was Arlington House (Figs 59 and 60). Opened in 1963, this multi-storey apartment block dominates Margate's skyline and its distinctive zigzag shape provides residents with spectacular views of the sea and coast. However, like many buildings of the 1960s it is both reviled and well loved, in the latter case by many of the people who live there.

Margate in the late 20th century

Guidebooks published in the 1960s painted a rosy picture of Margate. Happy families enjoyed warm sunshine and fun on clean beaches, and by the mid-1960s Arlington House was being featured as a good reason to live in Margate. Although everything seemed optimistic on the surface, the Borough Council was already conscious of the need for change. In 1965 it published its 'Central Area Redevelopment Scheme', which proposed radical solutions to prevent the town becoming: 'a solid mass of metal as traffic congests the narrow roads of the Borough'.[17] Improved

Figure 59 *There is great affection towards Arlington House from some of those closely associated with it, though the same cannot be said of the near-derelict retail square to the east and the car park to the south of the flats. [AA050590]*

Figure 60 *Arlington House's zig-zag elevations create a sort of internal balcony, which not only enhance the views from the flats, but also create a sensation of projecting out from the building. [DP032144]*

roads and car parking were needed, but to achieve this the local authority was prepared to forfeit some of its most important heritage. One of the car parks would have covered the Market Place and most of the old town, demonstrating that it was seen as having no relevance to the future of Margate. A purpose-built civic centre and a pedestrianised shopping area were to be provided on the south side of Cecil Square. The 1965 report boasted that:

> For both residents and visitors there will be modern highways, smoothing the way of motorists through the borough. There will be a bright and colourful shopping complex designed for comfort and convenience. Light and air will be let into the town centre, with the new

Figure 61 *Cecil Square provided entertainment and accommodation for holidaymakers for nearly 200 years; however, the redevelopment of the south-east corner focused on providing services for the local community. The Hippodrome was demolished in 1967 and was replaced by a lending library and local authority offices. [AA050560]*

civic centre and its surrounding flower beds and gardens . . . For the first time Margate will have a heart.[18]

The old town and Cecil Square had both enjoyed the role of being at Margate's 'heart' at different times, yet these precious historic assets would have suffered in the name of new development. By 1972, the first phase of the scheme was in progress (Fig 61), but phase 2, which involved the reshaping of the area around the Town Hall, did not take place as funding was not forthcoming. Instead, a revised plan was published which envisaged that the old town and harbour area, along with Dreamland and much of Marine Drive, would be designated for comprehensive redevelopment and improvement. This uncertainty about the future of the old town led to a decline in investment, which was exacerbated by more widespread economic decline in the 1980s.

By the end of the 20th century Margate, like many other English seaside resorts, was proving to be economically vulnerable, with a range of social problems. The heavy reliance on a declining industry, combined with low levels of employment in other sectors, such as manufacturing and information technology, led to a decline in the population and a shift towards an elderly demographic. The money being brought into Margate during the high season no longer covered the expenditure being incurred during the quieter low season. Investment in upgrading accommodation and improving attractions was reduced, resulting in facilities that were becoming outdated and even shabby (Figs 62 and 63). A survey of

Figure 62 *Located on the wall in the caretaker's office at Arlington House, this drawing conveys an impression of the sophisticated, modern shopping experience in Arlington Square in the 1960s. [Courtesy of Arlington House DP032122]*

Figure 63 *Arlington Square in 2007 – compare this modern reality with the idealistic vision of it from the 1960s in Figure 62. [DP032166]*

Figure 64 *Ye Olde Town Launderette, King Street, provides a stark reminder of the vulnerability of historic buildings in areas suffering difficult economic circumstances. [DP032060]*

Figure 65 *Taken on Whitsun Bank Holiday 1964, this amateur photograph captures a group of scooter-riding Mods on The Parade. Following national coverage of the trouble between Mods and Rockers, the Mayor of Margate was less than impressed with the adverse publicity: 'We in seaside resorts have a difficult enough job to make a living in the short English summer, and the sort of publicity we get from activities of these morons as glamorized in the national press and on television does us no good at all.' (The Times, Wednesday, 20 May 1964) [Unpublished amateur photograph]*

unlisted buildings in the old town revealed only 13 per cent were in a satisfactory condition, while for listed buildings the situation was worse, with fewer than 10 per cent being considered satisfactory (Fig 64). Margate had a poor image and had become synonymous with a low-budget, downmarket break (Fig 65). By around 2000, coach-based holiday operators reported that their elderly customers felt vulnerable and found Margate to be in a poor condition with inadequate facilities.

CHAPTER 3

A future for Margate

Towns have to change to survive. This may be by rapid expansion, exploiting new economic opportunities; at other times it may involve decline, dereliction and decay. The speed of change varies; what appears to be a long period of expansion and success can be followed by a subsequent decline that seems more rapid. Managing this cycle to prolong success and reverse decline is challenging. It requires an appreciation of the features that make a place distinctive and an understanding of why change happens. Towns have to balance strengthening their identity and retaining what is valued, with renewing some of their fabric and facilities.

Seaside resorts can be viewed as a type of industrial town whose main product has faced stiff competition from new foreign markets. European resorts could offer sunshine, warm seas and modern facilities, yet they provided holidays that were as cheap or cheaper than the traditional British seaside holiday. All resorts in Britain have suffered as a result, but Margate seems to have faced greater problems than most. Wartime damage and the post-war dilapidation seem to have made it particularly vulnerable in the late 20th century. In addition, problems caused by the car, and a poor media image, meant that by the start of the new millennium Margate's future seemed bleak. However, in the early 21st century there are signs of new initiatives that value the character of the town and its heritage, and that are seeking to build on these qualities to guarantee its future.

Margate in the 21st century

By the end of the 20th century, attempts had been made to address some of the symptoms of decline. The importance of the historic environment had been recognised by the decision to extend the Conservation Area. In the 1990s two Conservation Area Partnership Grant Schemes were instituted and in 1999 the development of an action plan for Margate's historic heart was undertaken. It included proposals for the regeneration of the old town and waterfront through the creation of an attractive and functional, historic quarter. Support would be provided to develop

Margate Sands, c1890–1910. Margate's gently sloping beach was a principal factor in its establishment as a health resort. Lined up at the edge of the high water mark, the phalanx of bathing machines continues a tradition that had been established at Margate around 150 years before. [OP00622]

innovative forms of economic activity, including arts businesses, and a new visitor attraction would be established, exploiting the association between Margate and one of its most famous past residents JMW Turner (Fig 66).

In 1994 the idea of a gallery to celebrate Turner's work was first proposed. It would also stage exhibitions by other artists connected with Kent, as well as shows featuring works by contemporary artists. A site beside the Droit House was identified and in 2003 a high-profile competition was won by Snøhetta and Spence Associates for a striking building adjacent to the stone pier, though technical difficulties with this scheme mean that a new design is currently being developed by David Chipperfield Architects (Fig 67). Although a building has not

Figure 66 (above) *The Old Town Gallery, located in a Grade II mid-19th-century building in Broad Street, suggests how the association with JMW Turner can be used to revitalise the old town. [DP023150]*

Figure 67 (left) *The Droit House was destroyed during the Second World War, but was reconstructed in 1947. The site adjacent to the Droit House may become the venue for Margate's new art gallery, the Turner Contemporary. [DP032201]*

yet appeared, several high-profile exhibitions of contemporary art have enjoyed considerable attention and have started the process of building a new image for Margate.

To improve the appearance of the seafront and to help build confidence in the town, Heritage Lottery monies were awarded to repair the seafront railings and start the process of investment in the public realm. An appreciation of the benefits of a high-quality historic environment in good repair led the council to bid for a Heritage Lottery Townscape Heritage Initiative (THI) Scheme. They were successful in 2002 and the Margate Old Town THI Scheme was launched with a common fund of £1,167,500 available over three years. This has led to the repair and refurbishment of a number of buildings that had been derelict for decades.

These modest beginnings in the old town may have helped to start the process of building new confidence in Margate, and further investment elsewhere seems to be occurring. A proposal for the former Marks and Spencer site in the High Street, with South East England Development Agency (SEEDA) investment, is being developed as a piece of modern and sensitive townscape. The Royal Sea Bathing Hospital to the west of Margate is in the process of renovation to provide high-quality apartments, and proposals are emerging for the regeneration of the Lido (Figs 68 and 69). A strategic urban design framework was produced in 2004 and an Action Plan for Margate was published in May 2005. However, a major project has yet to be delivered, and there is a danger that community support could fade if the momentum is not maintained. Nevertheless, there is now a better understanding of the aspirations for individual parts of the town, though there is still a need for an overarching vision that will bring the different elements together.

That vision should be to regenerate Margate by re-using its legacy of historic buildings. It has a wealth of fine buildings ranging from late-medieval timber-framed houses to the fine terraces and squares of the Georgian and Victorian eras. With suitable investment in sensitive refurbishment, using high-quality and appropriate materials, empty buildings can be turned into desirable homes and business premises.

Figure 68 *The Royal Sea Bathing Hospital is shown undergoing extensive redevelopment to convert the buildings into apartments. [DP032157]*

Figure 69 *The illuminated beacon for Margate Lido cunningly utilised the surviving chimney from the 19th-century Clifton Baths. [AA046224]*

Figure 70 These refurbished Georgian buildings on the Parade are providing high-quality accommodation for businesses, including a café with seating in the summer on the paved terrace in front. [AA050540]

Reviving the old town as a distinctive arts and cultural quarter, and using the intimate scale of the historic buildings as an attraction for new businesses, could once again allow the heart of the Margate to thrive (Fig 70). The first new businesses are already appearing in refurbished buildings and a former Lloyds Bank in King Street has been converted into the Margate Media Centre, providing a base for media-related companies seeking office accommodation.

The designation of a Housing Renewal Area in Cliftonville will help with the repair of its stock of handsome Victorian housing, addressing past neglect and unsympathetic subdivision. This could provide the type of elegant housing desired by a new community employed in the design and media businesses emerging in the old town. It would also restore the historic, functional links between the two areas and provide encouragement for a better-quality shopping centre. The regeneration of the Lido and Dreamland is currently under consideration, offering Margate a golden opportunity to improve its visitor 'offer' as a year-round destination.

With emerging concerns about the environmental impact of foreign travel, Margate could, with focus and drive, once again become a popular place to visit in the 21st century. Through rediscovering its colourful history and the buildings that tell this story, there is an opportunity for Margate to celebrate its distinctive heritage as one of the first and most important holiday resorts in England.

Notes

1   Camden, W 1806 *Britannia*. London: John Stockdale, 316

2   Chandler, J 1993 *John Leland's Itinerary*. Stroud: Sutton, 254; Cates, M and Chamberlain, D (eds) 1997 *The Maritime Heritage of Thanet*. Ramsgate: East Kent Maritime Trust, 45

3   Macky, J 1714 *A Journey through England*. Volume I, 50; Lewis, J 1736 *The History and Antiquities, as well Ecclesiastical and Civil, of the Isle of Tenet, in Kent*. London, 123

4   The Kentish Post or Canterbury News Letter 14 July 1736 cited in J Whyman 1985 *The Early Kentish Seaside: (1736–1840): selected documents* (Kentish Sources **8**). Gloucester: Sutton for Kent Archives Office, 160.

5   Anderson, J 1795 *A Practical Essay on the Good and Bad Effects of Sea-water and Sea-bathing*. London: C Dilly, 32

6   Anon 1765 *A Description of the Isle of Thanet*. London, 11

7   Anon 1770 *The Margate Guide*. London, 15

8   Anon 1760 'The Margate Ballad' *Universal Magazine* **27**, 324

9   Cozens, Z 1793 *A Tour through the Isle of Thanet, and some other parts of East Kent, etc*. London, 3

10 Anon 1810 *A Guide to all the Watering and Sea Bathing Places*. London, 304

11 Keate, G 1779 *Sketches from Nature; Taken, and Coloured, in a Journey to Margate*. London: J. Dodsley, Volume I, 104–5

12 Lyons, J A 1763 *A Description of the Isle of Thanet, and particularly of the town of Margate; … *. London, 15

13 Kidd, W 1831 *The Picturesque Pocket Companion to Margate, Ramsgate, Broadstairs, and the parts adjacent … *. London: William Kidd, 66

14 Anon 1899–1900 *Guide to Margate*. London: Ward, Lock and Co, 13

15 Anon 1899-1900 *Guide to Margate*, 8

16 'Seaside Change War-Time Decay At Margate, Holiday Memories In A Deserted Resort', *The Times*, 31 August 1943, 2

17 Sewell, G E 1965, *Borough of Margate Central Area Redevelopment Scheme 1965–80* (unpublished report)

18 Ibid

Further reading

Anon 1999 *Margate Old Town Action Plan: Space Syntax Research Paper 2*. University College London

Brodie, A and Winter, G 2007 *England's Seaside Resorts*. London: English Heritage

Brodie, A, Sargent, A and Winter, G 2005 *Seaside Holidays in the Past*. London: English Heritage

DLA Architecture and Waterbridge, 2006. *Dreamland Margate Feasibility Study Stage 2*

Humphries, R 1991 *Thanet at War 1939–45*. Stroud: Alan Sutton

Kent County Council, 1999 *A Turner Centre for Kent*

Locum Consulting, 2006 *Margate Destination Strategy*

Mason, T 2001 *Dreaming with Open Eyes: A Report on the Cultural Content and Focus of a Proposed Turner Centre for Margate* (report produced for Kent County Council)

Mirams, D 1984 *Old Margate*. Rainham: Meresborough Books

St Clair Strange, F G 1991 *The History of the Royal Sea Bathing Hospital, Margate 1791–1991*. Rainham: Meresborough Books

Scurrell, D 1982 *The Book of Margate*. Buckingham: Barracuda

Sewell, G E 1965 *Borough of Margate Central Area Redevelopment Scheme 1965–80* (unpublished report)

Sewell, G E 1972 *Margate Central Area Redevelopment Proposals Third Report*

Whyman, J 1985 *The Early Kentish Seaside: 1736–1840 Selected Documents*. Gloucester: Alan Sutton for Kent Archives Office

Other titles in the Informed Conservation series

Behind the Veneer: The South Shoreditch furniture trade and its buildings.
Joanna Smith and Ray Rogers, 2006.
Product code 51204, ISBN 9781873592960

The Birmingham Jewellery Quarter: An introduction and guide.
John Cattell and Bob Hawkins, 2000.
Product code 50204, ISBN 9781850747772

Bridport and West Bay: The buildings of the flax and hemp industry.
Mike Williams, 2006.
Product code 51167, ISBN 9781873592861

Built to Last? The buildings of the Northamptonshire boot and shoe industry.
Kathryn A Morrison with Ann Bond, 2004.
Product code 50921, ISBN 9781873592793

Gateshead: Architecture in a changing English urban landscape.
Simon Taylor and David Lovie, 2004.
Product code 52000, ISBN 9781873592762

Religion and Place in Leeds.
John Minnis and Trevor Mitchell, 2007.
Product code 51337, ISBN 9781905624485

Manchester's Northern Quarter.
Simon Taylor and Julian Holder, 2007.
Product code 50946, ISBN 9781873592847

Manchester: The warehouse legacy – An introduction and guide.
Simon Taylor, Malcolm Cooper and P S Barnwell, 2002.
Product code 50668, ISBN 9781873592670

Newcastle's Grainger Town: An urban renaissance.
Fiona Cullen and David Lovie, 2003.
Product code 50811, ISBN 9781873592779

'One Great Workshop': The buildings of the Sheffield metal trades.
Nicola Wray, Bob Hawkins and Colum Giles, 2001.
Product code 50214, ISBN 9781873592663

Storehouses of Empire: Liverpool's historic warehouses.
Colum Giles and Bob Hawkins, 2004.
Product code 50920, ISBN 9781873592809

Stourport-on-Severn: Pioneer town of the canal age.
Colum Giles, Keith Falconer, Barry Jones and Michael Taylor.
Product code 51290, ISBN 9781905624362

£7.99 each (plus postage and packing)

To order
Tel: EH Sales 01761 452966
Email: ehsales@gillards.com

Online bookshop: www.english-heritage.org.uk

Gazetteer of Margate's principal buildings of interest

(1) Former Royal Sea Bathing Hospital
Built in 1792–6 to provide sea-bathing facilities for patients with scrofula, the building was extended during the mid- and late 19th century (*see* Figs 21, 22, 23 and 68).

(2) Sea View Terrace
Sea View Terrace is one of Margate's least-spoilt sea-front terraces. The hooded, cast-iron balconies and canted bays give this mid-Victorian terrace a welcome uniformity (*see* Fig 37).

(3) Royal Crescent
Royal Crescent was built in the 1850s, and according to the 1861 census it comprised private dwellings and lodging houses. By the end of the 19th century, the three houses at the eastern end had been converted into a hotel (*see* Fig 35).

(4) Buenos Ayres
Originating from 1803, though still incomplete in 1821, Buenos Ayres was the earliest development near the Royal Sea Bathing Hospital. In the early 19th century the terrace was apparently used as lodging houses (*see* Figs 27 and 28).

(5) Bathing Pool, Marine Sands
The tidal Bathing Pool opened in 1937 on the seaward side of the 1926 Marine Terrace Bathing Pavilion (demolished in 1990). This allowed people to swim in seawater, regardless of the state of the tide.

(6) Arlington House and Square
Designed by Russell Diplock Associates and opened in 1963, it stands on the site of the former South Eastern Railway station. Being perpendicular to the seafront allows all the flats to have views of the coast (*see* Figs 59, 60, 62 and 63).

(7) Dreamland
Dreamland Amusement Park was the principal attraction between the wars. The Scenic Railway, constructed in 1919–20, is the oldest surviving rollercoaster in Great Britain, and one of only two surviving scenic railways, hence its Grade II listing. The front of the complex is dominated by the cinema, which opened in 1935 (*see* Figs 46, 51, 52 and 53).

(8) Marine Terrace
From 1809 'The New Road' was built along the seafront between the western edge of Margate and Buenos Ayres. Houses were added during the first half of the 19th century.

(9) Albert Terrace houses
The northern end of Albert Terrace, which stood on the seafront prior to the construction of Marine Drive, is an eclectic mix of houses built during the first half of the 19th century.

(10) Marine Drive
In October 1878, work commenced on Marine Drive connecting the Parade with Marine Terrace by reclaiming land on the seaward side of High Street. This work was completed in 1880 (*see* Fig 43).

(11) Site of Circulating Library and Imperial Hotel
The New Marine Library was rebuilt on the site of an earlier library, swept away by the 1808 storm. The new, three-storied building consisted of a large block with an attached rotunda and a projecting gallery (*see* Fig 7). The Imperial Hotel was built on this site in 1880.

(12) Site of Bathing Rooms, High Street
Six larger bathing rooms were built to replace those destroyed in 1808. They provided individual baths, showers, and waiting rooms for people wishing to use bathing machines in the sea below (*see* Figs 6, 7 and 8).

(13) Grosvenor Place Houses
Formerly known as The Rope Walk, this was one of the popular promenades. Rows of terraced houses facing west towards the Margate Brook were added during the 19th century.

(14) Former Cinema de Luxe, High Street
Built in 1914–15, though its interior was altered in 1936, this early, purpose-built cinema was designed by Peter Dulvey Stoneham. It closed as a cinema in 1987.

(15) Hawley Square
Margate's second square, begun *c*1770, was 'nearly completed' in 1790, by which time a series of houses, boarding houses, the theatre and library had been built (*see* Figs 16, 17, 18, 19 and 20).

(16) Site of Circulating Library
In 1786 a combined library and shop was built on the north-west corner of Hawley Square. The present building was erected in 1931 for the Thanet School of Arts and Crafts (*see* Figs 16, 17 and 19).

(17) Theatre Royal
The Theatre Royal was built in 1786–7. It was remodelled in 1874 by Jethro Thomas Robinson, designer of the Old Vic and father-in-law of the prolific theatre architect Frank Matcham (*see* Fig 20).

(18) Union Crescent
Erected in 1799, Union Crescent was Margate's first crescent. It is a regular terrace of ten tall, brick houses, which for much of their early existence provided lodgings for visitors (*see* Figs 31 and 32).

(19) Cecil Square
Built in 1769 as a new centre for the growing resort, the houses were intended 'for the reception of the nobility and gentry' and therefore imitated the latest fashions in London's newest suburbs (*see* Figs 12, 13, 14, 15 and 30).

(20) Site of the Royal Hotel and Assembly Rooms and the Grand Theatre
At the southern corner of Cecil Square, a large assembly room was built in around 1769. It was destroyed by fire in 1882, and was replaced by the New Theatre, which opened in 1898. Later renamed the Grand Theatre, then The Hippodrome, it was demolished in 1967. The courts, library and local authority offices now occupy the site (*see* Figs 14, 15 and 61).

(21) 13 Cecil Square
This house is said to have been occupied by the Duke of Cumberland. As befits the home of a member of the Royal Family, a pediment distinguishes it from the other houses around the square (*see* Figs 13 and 15).

(22) Site of Circulating Library, Cecil Street
Samuel Silver moved into this new library in 1783. It contained a library and shop, as well as hosting card games and musical performances (*see* Fig 15).

(23) India House, Hawley Street

Described by John Newman as 'the best house in Margate', India House was built in *c*1767. It is unlike any other 18th-century building in Margate, resembling a bungalow, itself an Indian-inspired form, as much a Georgian house (*see* Fig 10).

(24) Town Hall

The Town Hall was built in 1820–1, in the centre of Market Place. New municipal offices were added in 1897–8 and a linking corridor was created at first-floor level to provide access between the buildings.

(25) The Parade

This curving stretch of land to the south of the harbour was a popular area for early visitors. It was probably the site of Thomas Barber's first baths and was the location of Mitchener's New Inn, the principal place of entertainment before Cecil Square was built (*see* Figs 25, 56, 57 and 70).

(26) Houses in King Street

King Street contains some of the town's oldest buildings. Tudor House is a 16th-century timber-framed house, while further west, houses with knapped-flint walls, brick dressings and shaped gables reveal something of the vernacular style (*see* Figs 2 and 3).

(27) Former Parade Cinema, The Parade

The Parade Cinema, built by C W Stanley and W J Ballard, opened in 1911. The façade has panels decorated with masks and musical instruments, suggesting that the building may have been conceived as a music hall (*see* Fig 50).

(28) The Pier

The pier was constructed in 1810–15 to designs by the engineers John Rennie and William Jessup. The Droit House, for collecting tolls, was built in 1812, and rebuilt in 1828 or 1830. It was destroyed during the Second World War and rebuilt in 1947 (*see* Figs 25, 26 and 67).

(29) Site of Pier Hotel and Hotel Metropole

In 1878, the Pier Hotel and Duke's Head Hotel were combined to form the Grand Hotel, but following a fire in 1890 this was rebuilt as the Hotel Metropole. This hotel and the adjacent Neptune Square area were demolished between 1937 and 1939 (*see* Figs 55 and 56).

(30) The Jetty

In 1824, Jarvis' Landing Place, for landing visitors from steamers, was constructed to the east of the pier. This wooden jetty was replaced in 1853–5 by Eugenius Birch's first seaside pier. A hexagonal pier head extension was added in 1875–7. In January 1978 the Jetty was largely destroyed in a storm (*see* Figs 44 and 45).

(31) Site of Marine Palace

The Marine Palace was built on an area of reclaimed land between the Jetty and Fort Point in 1876. It included two swimming baths, an aquarium, a ballroom, a billiard room and a skating rink. The building was destroyed by a storm in 1897.

(32) Trinity Square, including site of Holy Trinity Church

Trinity Square was a piecemeal development of terraced houses on three sides of an irregular 'square'. Holy Trinity Church (1825–8) in its centre was damaged in a bombing raid in 1943 and was later demolished (*see* Fig 58).

(33) Fort Crescent

Fort Crescent was laid out as a planned, cliff-top crescent in the early 19th century, but only three properties had been constructed by 1821. Temeraire Court, originally Fort Lodge, is an unusual house because its form is derived from Brighton rather than London models (*see* Fig 33).

(34) The Winter Gardens

The Winter Gardens was constructed in 1910–11 in a hole excavated into the cliff. During the Second World War the Winter Gardens acted as a receiving station for troops evacuated from Dunkirk and was damaged during a bombing raid in 1941 (*see* Fig 49).

(35) Fort Paragon

Built in 1830, this terrace of houses was built by a local builder, Harold Woodward, who was also responsible for part of Marine Terrace (*see* Fig 34).

(36) Clifton Baths and Lido

Clifton Baths were created by excavating into the cliffs at the Fort. The complex originally consisted of a dwelling-house, warm and cold baths, dressing rooms, and a reading room. The tidal pool was created beside the baths in 1927 and renamed the Lido in the 1930s (*see* Figs 54 and 69).

(37) Ethelbert Crescent and the site of the Cliftonville Hotel

The Cliftonville Hotel (1868) was the centrepiece of Ethelbert Crescent. It contained 300 rooms, but with the decline in the popularity of large hotels at seaside resorts it ceased to be economically viable. Its site is now occupied by a bowling alley, night club and café (*see* Figs 36, 40 and 41).

(38) Dalby Square

The three-sided 'square', open at the seaward end to provide sea views, was a common feature at seaside resorts in the 19th century. The flanking terraces of Dalby Square are among the grandest houses built at Margate (*see* Figs 38 and 39).

(39) Former Princess Mary's Hospital

East Cliff Home was founded in 1895 as a convalescent home for poor children suffering from pulmonary tuberculosis. In 1929–30 it was converted into a convalescent home for women and in *c*1938 a new, large, U-shaped dormitory block was built. In 1984, the main buildings were converted into a nursing home.

(40) The Shell Grotto

The Grotto consists of two semicircular passages leading to a central dome, from which a passage leads to a rectangular chamber. It was probably created in the mid-18th century, perhaps as a private amusement, or as a curiosity for some of Margate's early visitors (*see* Fig 11).

(41) Royal School for Deaf Children Margate, Victoria Road

The school opened in 1875, and by 1880 it could educate 240 children. The imposing, but institutional, buildings were demolished in 1971 and replaced by a complex that resembles a modern school.

Map of Margate showing the location of the buildings mentioned in the gazetteer

KEY

1 Former Royal Sea Bathing Hospital
2 Sea View Terrace
3 Royal Crescent
4 Buenos Ayres
5 Bathing Pool, Marine Sands
6 Arlington House and Square
7 Dreamland
8 Marine Terrace
9 Albert Terrace houses
10 Marine Drive
11 Site of Circulating Library and Imperial Hotel
12 Site of Bathing Rooms, High Street
13 Grosvenor Place Houses
14 Former Cinema de Luxe, High Street
15 Hawley Square
16 Site of Circulating Library
17 Theatre Royal
18 Union Crescent
19 Cecil Square
20 Site of the Royal Hotel and Assembly Rooms and the Grand Theatre
21 13 Cecil Square
22 Site of Circulating Library, Cecil Street
23 India House, Hawley Street
24 Town Hall
25 The Parade
26 Houses in King Street
27 Former Parade Cinema, The Parade
28 The Pier
29 Site of Pier Hotel and Hotel Metropole
30 The Jetty
31 Site of Marine Palace
32 Trinity Square, including site of Holy Trinity Church
33 Fort Crescent
34 The Winter Gardens
35 Fort Paragon
36 Clifton Baths and Lido
37 Ethelbert Crescent and the site of the Cliftonville Hotel
38 Dalby Square
39 Former Princess Mary's Hospital
40 The Shell Grotto
41 Royal School for Deaf Children Margate, Victoria Road

Back cover
Margate from Arlington House. [DP03213]